Racing to the Future

Before You Read

The story begins in Shanghai, a major city located in the central section of China's east coast, and then moves around 1,200 km to the north to Beijing, the nation's capital. From there, the story takes us to Hebei, a **province**[1] which surrounds Beijing, and on to Shenyang, a city that is close to 700 km northeast of Beijing. The story picks up in Beijing again, heading northwest to Zhangjiakou and then west to Hohhot, Inner Mongolia. It continues further west to Baotou and then finally southwest to Lanzhou in the far west of China. Other cities mentioned are Changsha, in south central China; Hefei, a city approximately 470 km west of Shanghai; and Fuzhou, a city located on the east coast of China, across from Taiwan and roughly midway between Shanghai and Shenzhen.

A. China Before Rail. Read the paragraph. Then complete the sentences with the correct forms of the underlined words.

Before rail was introduced, the primary means of transportation in China was by boat, often along China's many great rivers, which include the Yellow River in the north, the Changjiang (known as the Yangtze River in English) in central China, and the Zhujiang in the south. People also used the Grand Canal, one of the glories of ancient China, which connected Beijing with Hangzhou, 1,776 kilometers to the south. Traveling long distance by road had many drawbacks, as there were mountains and rivers to cross, and the roads were sometimes poor. The sheer difficulty made it unpopular, but when people did travel long distance by land they often walked, or rode donkeys or horses. Carriages were not very common, though rich people sometimes used them. Transporting goods over land was most often accomplished by donkey or camel.

1. We were impressed by the new railways station. It is such a _____ and beautiful building that it outshined all the buildings around it.
2. The train was so fast that we _____ our trip in less than four hours.
3. While we would like to travel there by car, it has too many _____. The train is just easier.
4. I'd like to travel in a _____ pulled by two white horses when I get married.
5. The trip through south China was simply _____—we saw so many wonderful things!
6. It was _____ joy to see the beautiful mountains from our train as it rushed through the countryside.

[1] **province**: a large district of a country

B. **High Speed Rail in China. Look at the table and look at the photos in this reader. Then answer the questions below.**

The Growth of High Speed Rail (HSR) in China					
Year	2009	2011	2013	2015	2017
HSR track (km)	2,699	6,601	11,028	19,838	25,164
HSR / total track (%)	3.2%	7.1%	10.7%	16.4%	19.8%
HSR passengers (millions)	46.5	285.5	529.6	961.4	1,752.2
HSR / total rail passengers (%)	3.1%	15.8%	25.1%	37.9%	56.8%

1. Have you ever ridden on a high speed train? What was it like?
2. What do you know about high speed trains in China?
3. Why do you think people might prefer riding high speed trains over other forms of transportation, such as plane or car?
4. What other countries have high speed rail? How might their high speed rail systems differ from that in China?

At 7 a.m., we boarded the state-of-the-art Fuxing Hao train at Shanghai Railway Station. We stored our bags at the front of the car, found our seats, and settled in. After some announcements in Chinese and English, the train slowly set off. I say "slowly" because that is exactly how it felt. Unlike other trains which start with a shake, this train accelerated so smoothly that if you were not looking out the windows, you could hardly tell we were moving. Yet, within minutes, we were passing over the rails at speeds of more than 350 kilometers an hour.

Track 1

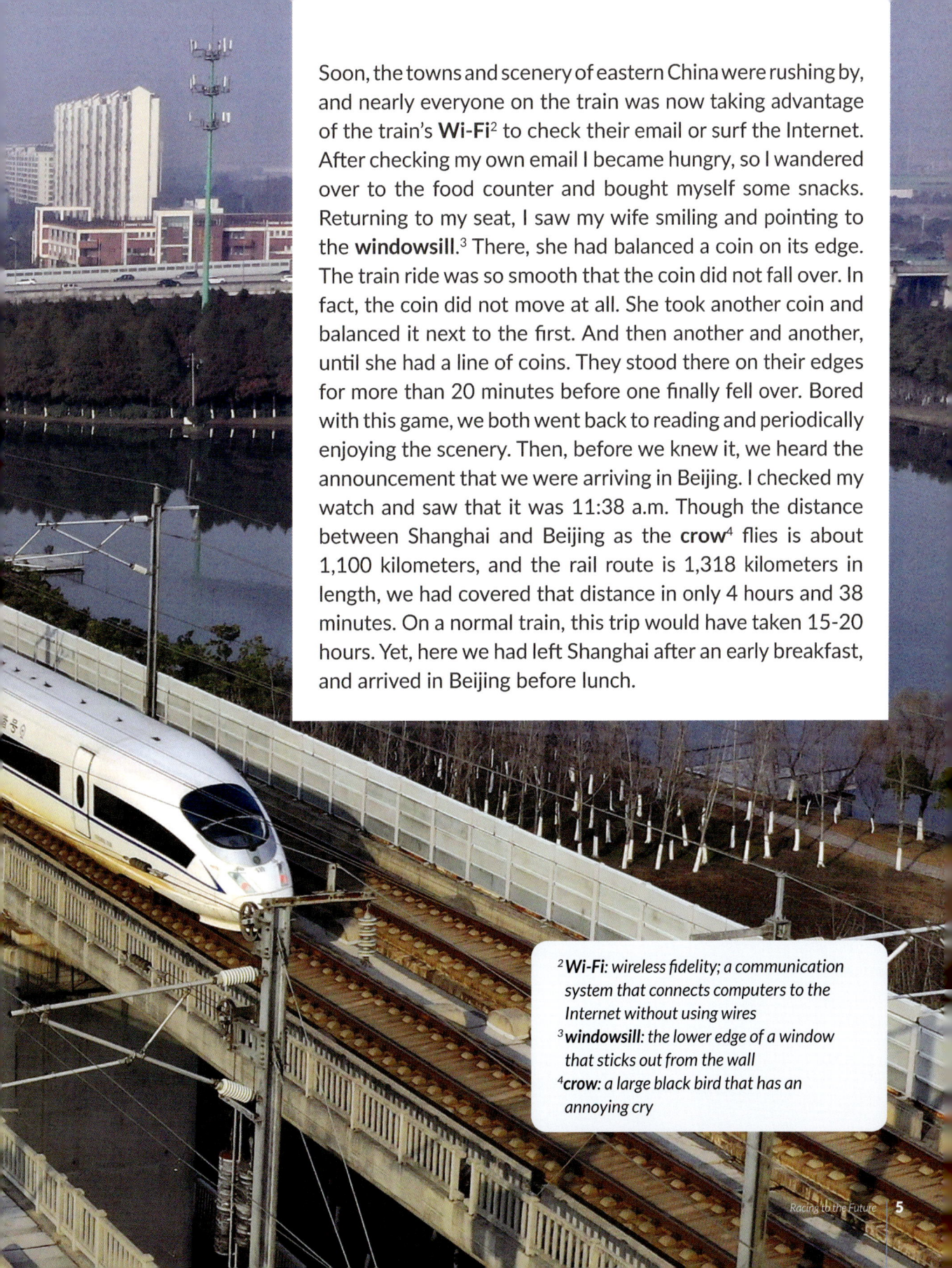

Soon, the towns and scenery of eastern China were rushing by, and nearly everyone on the train was now taking advantage of the train's **Wi-Fi**[2] to check their email or surf the Internet. After checking my own email I became hungry, so I wandered over to the food counter and bought myself some snacks. Returning to my seat, I saw my wife smiling and pointing to the **windowsill**.[3] There, she had balanced a coin on its edge. The train ride was so smooth that the coin did not fall over. In fact, the coin did not move at all. She took another coin and balanced it next to the first. And then another and another, until she had a line of coins. They stood there on their edges for more than 20 minutes before one finally fell over. Bored with this game, we both went back to reading and periodically enjoying the scenery. Then, before we knew it, we heard the announcement that we were arriving in Beijing. I checked my watch and saw that it was 11:38 a.m. Though the distance between Shanghai and Beijing as the **crow**[4] flies is about 1,100 kilometers, and the rail route is 1,318 kilometers in length, we had covered that distance in only 4 hours and 38 minutes. On a normal train, this trip would have taken 15-20 hours. Yet, here we had left Shanghai after an early breakfast, and arrived in Beijing before lunch.

[2] **Wi-Fi**: *wireless fidelity; a communication system that connects computers to the Internet without using wires*
[3] **windowsill**: *the lower edge of a window that sticks out from the wall*
[4] **crow**: *a large black bird that has an annoying cry*

Li Hongzhang (front row, 4th from left) and other high-ranking officials inspecting the Tangshan-Xugezhuang railway line in 1881

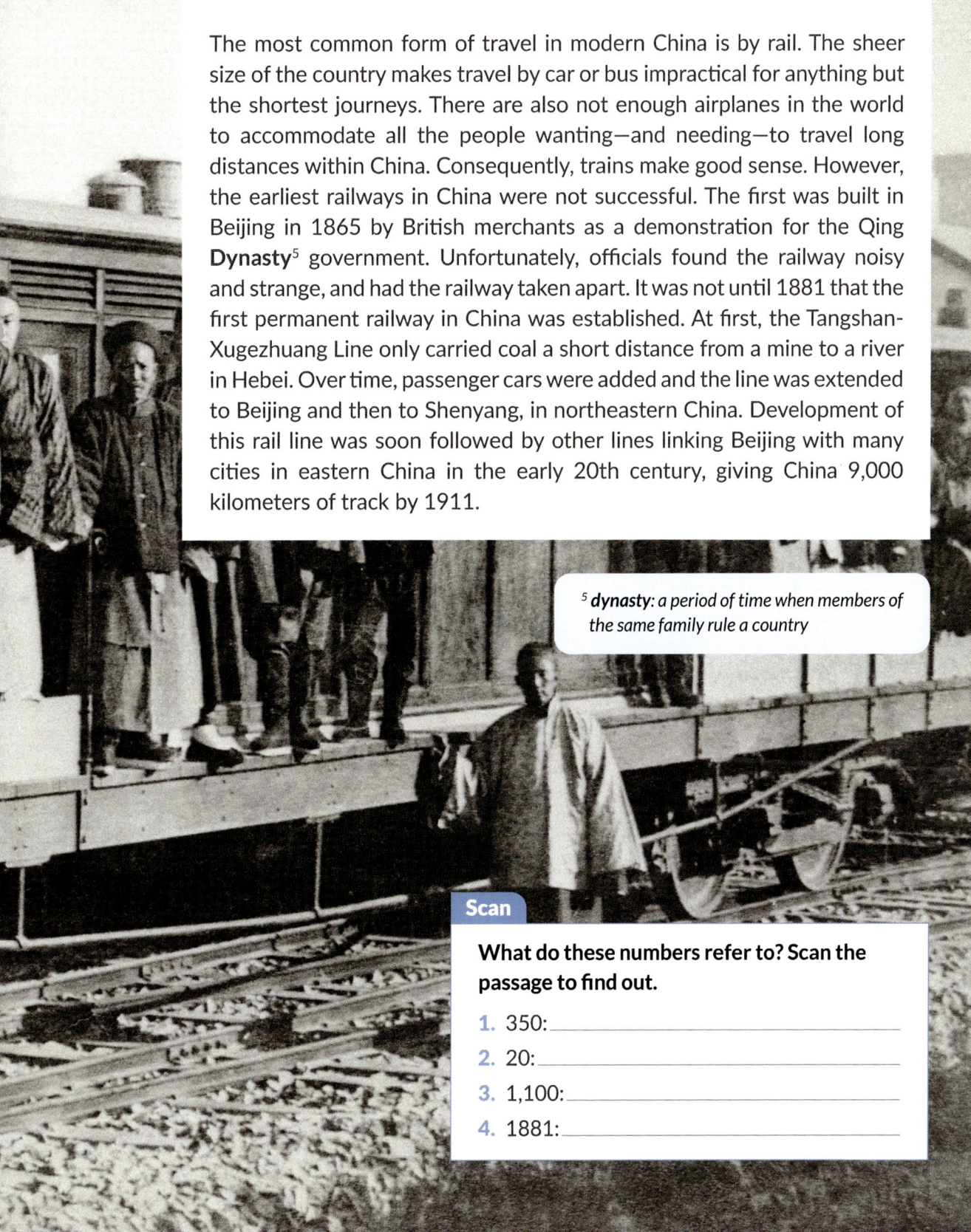

The most common form of travel in modern China is by rail. The sheer size of the country makes travel by car or bus impractical for anything but the shortest journeys. There are also not enough airplanes in the world to accommodate all the people wanting—and needing—to travel long distances within China. Consequently, trains make good sense. However, the earliest railways in China were not successful. The first was built in Beijing in 1865 by British merchants as a demonstration for the Qing **Dynasty**[5] government. Unfortunately, officials found the railway noisy and strange, and had the railway taken apart. It was not until 1881 that the first permanent railway in China was established. At first, the Tangshan-Xugezhuang Line only carried coal a short distance from a mine to a river in Hebei. Over time, passenger cars were added and the line was extended to Beijing and then to Shenyang, in northeastern China. Development of this rail line was soon followed by other lines linking Beijing with many cities in eastern China in the early 20th century, giving China 9,000 kilometers of track by 1911.

[5] *dynasty: a period of time when members of the same family rule a country*

Scan

What do these numbers refer to? Scan the passage to find out.

1. 350: _____
2. 20: _____
3. 1,100: _____
4. 1881: _____

Zhan Tianyou (front row, 8th from left) at the opening ceremony of Beijing-Zhangjiakou railway line on November 2, 1909

One important early rail line was the Beijing-Zhangjiakou line, completed in 1909, which connected Beijing with the city of Zhangjiakou, about 200 kilometers to the northwest. Other rail lines then under development used Western financing and assistance, but Zhangjiakou was an important trading post with Russia and the Chinese government felt the line was a high priority, so it decided that construction should be all-Chinese, and headed up by a Chinese engineer. Hence, Zhan Tianyou (1861-1919) was given this important job. Zhan had been born in Guangdong, but when he was twelve years old, he was sent by the government to study in the USA, where he graduated from high school and then attended Yale University to study engineering. He received a **Ph.B.**[6] in 1881. On his return to China, he gained experience working on the railroad between Beijing and Shenyang, before being given the responsibility of building the Beijing-Zhangjiakou line. Through his skill, many technical difficulties were overcome and the railroad was completed two years ahead of schedule, earning Zhan the nickname the Father of Chinese Railroads, which was used inside and outside China.

As the 20th century progressed, new lines were built, and existing rail lines were lengthened. For example, the Beijing-Zhangjiakou line was extended 300 kilometers to Hohhot, Inner Mongolia by 1921, and then another 186 kilometers to Baotou by 1923. Development of the Chinese rail network, however, was soon stalled by war.

[6] **Ph.B.:** *an advanced university degree*

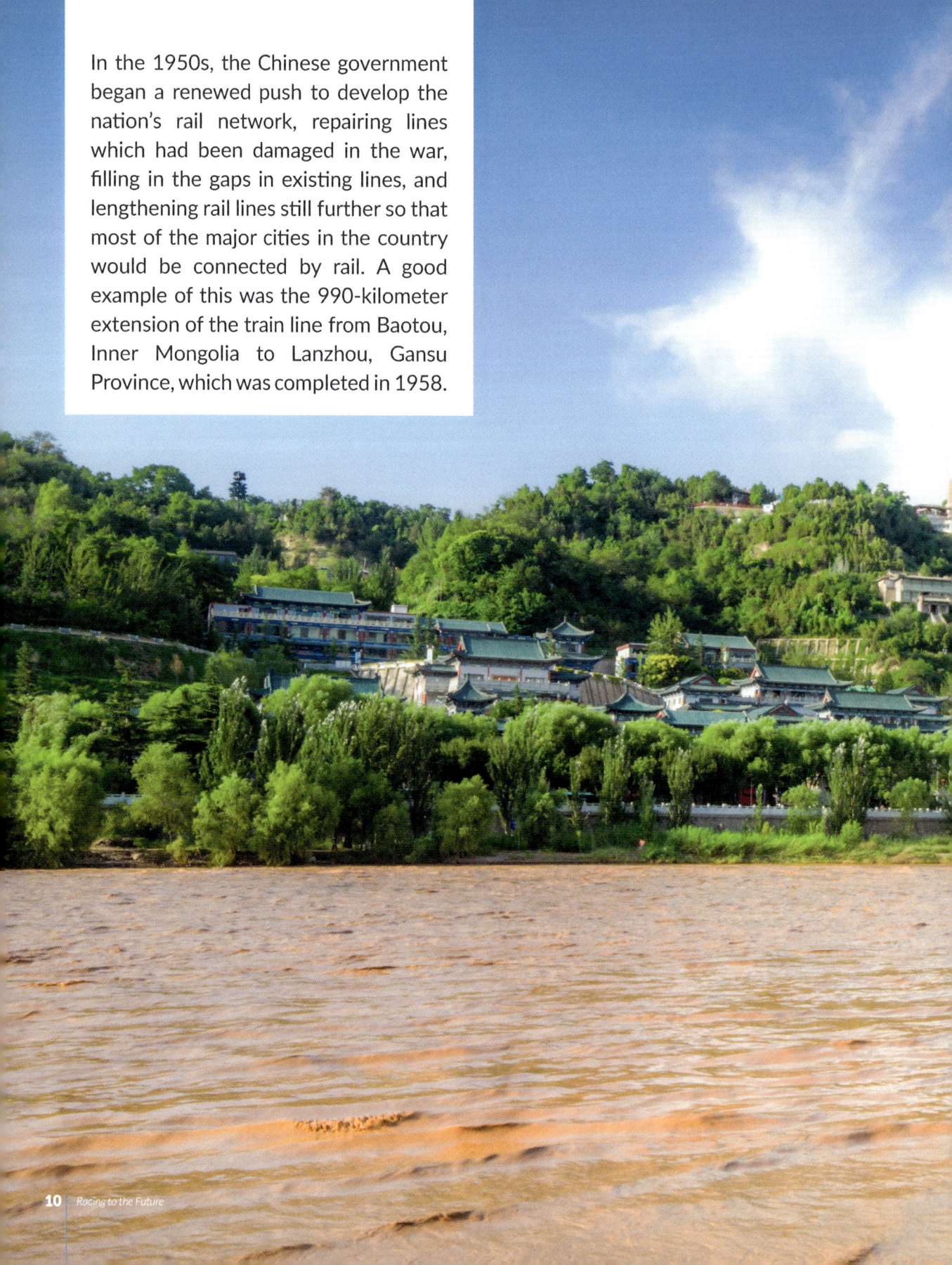

In the 1950s, the Chinese government began a renewed push to develop the nation's rail network, repairing lines which had been damaged in the war, filling in the gaps in existing lines, and lengthening rail lines still further so that most of the major cities in the country would be connected by rail. A good example of this was the 990-kilometer extension of the train line from Baotou, Inner Mongolia to Lanzhou, Gansu Province, which was completed in 1958.

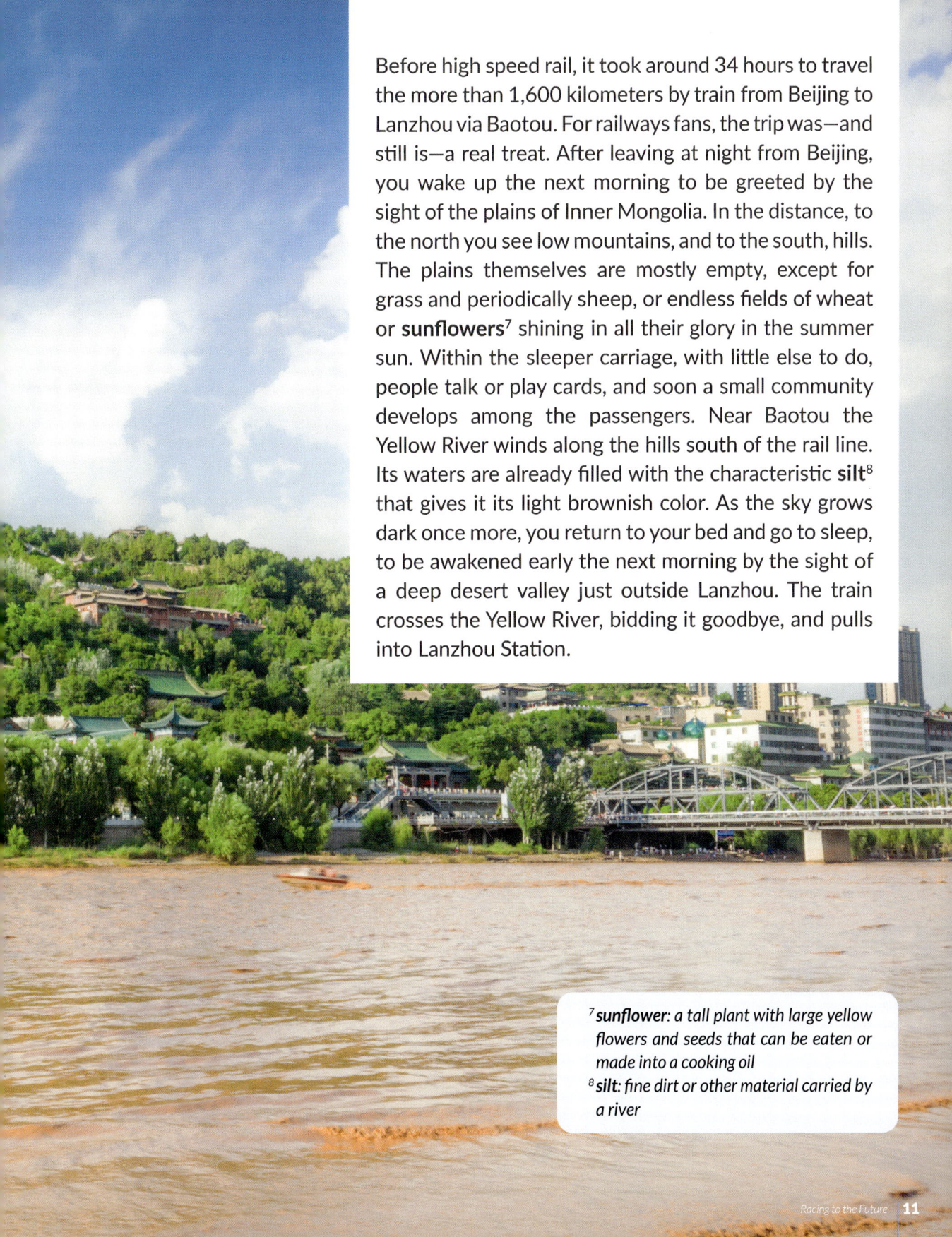

Before high speed rail, it took around 34 hours to travel the more than 1,600 kilometers by train from Beijing to Lanzhou via Baotou. For railways fans, the trip was—and still is—a real treat. After leaving at night from Beijing, you wake up the next morning to be greeted by the sight of the plains of Inner Mongolia. In the distance, to the north you see low mountains, and to the south, hills. The plains themselves are mostly empty, except for grass and periodically sheep, or endless fields of wheat or **sunflowers**[7] shining in all their glory in the summer sun. Within the sleeper carriage, with little else to do, people talk or play cards, and soon a small community develops among the passengers. Near Baotou the Yellow River winds along the hills south of the rail line. Its waters are already filled with the characteristic **silt**[8] that gives it its light brownish color. As the sky grows dark once more, you return to your bed and go to sleep, to be awakened early the next morning by the sight of a deep desert valley just outside Lanzhou. The train crosses the Yellow River, bidding it goodbye, and pulls into Lanzhou Station.

[7] *sunflower: a tall plant with large yellow flowers and seeds that can be eaten or made into a cooking oil*
[8] *silt: fine dirt or other material carried by a river*

A trip like this is very much part of the romance of train travel—many people spend their lives dreaming of taking trips like this as a part of a grand adventure. The problem is the sheer amount of time such a journey can take when you are not looking for adventure, but simply need to get from one place to another for work or school.

In a country the size of China it was often quite time-consuming to get from one place to another, with many rail journeys taking more than 30 hours. And while it can be quite enjoyable to take a long journey by train, such time-consuming rail journeys are not practical for a rapidly developing country with millions of people constantly on the move. For this reason, it was absolutely necessary to develop a high speed rail system.

An early attempt to find a technological breakthrough for high speed rail travel in China was the Shanghai **Maglev**,[9] which opened to the public in 2004. The first commercial magnetic-**levitation**[10] train in the world, it connects Shanghai's Pudong International Airport with the Shanghai subway system, traveling a distance of 30 kilometers in 8 minutes, at speeds as high as 430 kilometers per hour. It is the fastest commercially operated train anywhere in the world. China now has two more maglevs, one in Changsha and the other in Beijing. However, both of these only cover short distances and the trains travel at speeds of around 100 kilometers per hour, which is not much faster than trains on many conventional rail lines. Apart from the complex technical and safety issues involved with maglev trains, the big drawback with having a maglev line appears to be the high cost. Thus, while maglev technology will continue to be used in the future—a train that is capable of reaching speeds of 600 kilometers per hour is being developed—the focus has been on more conventional, off-the-shelf technology in the development of China's high speed rail network.

[9] **maglev**: magnetic-levitation; a transport system in which trains use magnets to travel over metal rails
[10] **levitation**: the rising and floating of something in the air without physical support

In 2007, what was then known as the Chinese Ministry of Railways began joint **ventures**[11] with four companies (from Canada, Japan, France, and Germany) to develop high speed rail within China. While the original technology was imported, as Chinese railway technology matured the development of the high speed rail system became increasingly localized, until the all-Chinese Fuxing Hao (**Renaissance**[12]) was created and rolled into production in 2017.

China now has nearly 30,000 kilometers of high speed track, and this is expected to extend to 38,000 kilometers by 2025. Fully two thirds of the world's high speed rail (by length) is in China, with trains traveling at an average of 200-300 kilometers per hour. Using high speed rail, what used to be a 34-hour journey between Beijing and Lanzhou can now be accomplished in just seven to nine hours. While this is still a long journey, it means you can leave in the morning and arrive in the late afternoon.

[11]**venture**: *a risky business deal*
[12]**renaissance**: *a time of rebirth, especially in music, art, and technology*

Infer Meaning

1. Why does a small community develop among the passengers on some long distance train journeys?
2. How did the Yellow River get its name?
3. In what way is a long distance train trip between Beijing and Lanzhou part of a grand adventure?

While the main draw of many of the high speed rail lines is convenience for people wanting to get from one city to another as quickly as possible, some of these high speed lines have become popular tourist attractions. A good example of this is the Hefei-Fuzhou high speed rail line, completed in 2015, which connects Hefei with Fuzhou, 813 kilometers away. Speed is certainly an appeal with this line—it cuts travel time from fourteen to four hours—but the main draw is the beautiful scenery. Technically speaking, this was one of the most challenging high speed rail routes ever built; nearly 90% of the track was laid either on bridges or in tunnels. However, the spectacular views are worth it, as the train winds its way through some of China's most beautiful mountainous areas, including the Huangshan and the Wuyi Mountain Ranges, and Sanqing Mountain.

Now that China has gained skill and knowledge in high speed rail, it is seeking to export its technology to other countries. Its first venture on the international market was the development of a new high speed rail line connecting Istanbul with Turkey's capital, Ankara, 530 kilometers away. This was followed by projects in Saudi Arabia, Hungary and Serbia, Thailand, and Indonesia, among other countries. Perhaps its most ambitious project is a Trans-Asian network linking China with Europe, which is hoped to be completed by 2030 as a part of China's Belt and Road Initiative. Already, China has agreed to build a 762-kilometer high speed rail line in Russia linking Moscow to Kazan.

While rail travel between China and Europe has been possible for over a century with links to the Trans-Siberian Express, the time involved has made it impractical when compared to modern air travel—from Beijing to Moscow alone it takes more than a week when traveling by train. However, using high speed rail, the time from Beijing to London could potentially be cut to two or three days, making high speed rail a fast and a cost-efficient way to travel between China and Europe.

Thanks to high speed rail, the travel time between major cities in China has already been reduced to only a few hours, making travel within China much more convenient, both for Chinese citizens and travelers from overseas. This convenience in turn should accelerate development within China, as the time and expense of long distance transportation has been greatly lowered. No doubt, it will also bring the people of the country closer together, and in time bring about deep social changes, the full nature of which no one can fully guess.

What Do You Think?

1. Why do you think the Beijing and Changsha maglev lines are much slower than the Shanghai Maglev?
2. What advantages might there be in taking a high speed train from Beijing to London rather than going by plane?
3. Which train journey would you most like to take in China? Why?

After You Read

A. **Multiple Choice.** Answer the questions below by choosing A, B, C, or D.

1. What does the phrase "as the crow flies" mean on page 5?
   A. by plane
   B. going the quickest way
   C. in a straight line
   D. using the highway

2. What would be a good heading for the paragraph on page 7?
   A. China's First Steps Towards Rail Travel
   B. The Story of the Tangshan-Xugezhuang Line
   C. Trains, a Noisy and Strange Invention
   D. China is a Big Country

3. According to the passage, what repays the effort of building the Hefei-Fuzhou line?
   A. the popularity of the line as a tourist attraction
   B. the spectacular views
   C. being able to travel quickly between the two cities
   D. the technical challenges

4. According to the passage, what is the most difficult high speed rail venture that China plans to take on?
   A. connecting the whole country with high speed rail
   B. building maglev trains
   C. designing and building its own trains
   D. a rail network connecting China with Europe

5. On page 18, the passage says, "No doubt, it will also bring the people of the country closer together." What does "it" refer to?
   A. the reduced travel time
   B. accelerated development within China
   C. the convenience of high speed rail
   D. the affordable cost of high speed rail

B. **Put Events in Order.** Put the events below in the order that they happened. Number them 1-8.

_____ The Chinese Ministry of Railways began joint ventures to develop high speed rail within China.

_____ The Tangshan-Xugezhuang Line was established.

_____ The Hefei-Fuzhou high speed rail line was completed.

_____ The Shanghai Maglev was opened to the public.

_____ The Beijing-Zhangjiakou line was completed.

_____ A railway was built by British merchants as a demonstration.

_____ The Baotou-Lanzhou Line was completed.

_____ The Fuxing Hao rolled into production.

C. **Answer the questions.** Use information from the passage to answer the questions below.

1. Apart from the speed, what impressed the author most about high speed train travel?
2. What are some reasons why Chinese prefer rail travel over other forms of transportation?
3. What does the failure of China's first train say about Qing Dynasty officials?
4. How do you prefer to travel? Why?

Railways on the Roof of the World

🎧 **Track 2**

By far, the most technologically challenging railway ever built was probably the Qinghai-Tibet Railway, completed in 2006, connecting Xining to Lhasa, 1,956 kilometers away. Fully 550 kilometers of this line are built on permafrost—frozen earth. The rail line is also by far the highest in the world: at Tanggula Pass it is 5,072 meters above sea level, and more than 960 kilometers of the line is above 4,000 meters. The railway was first planned in the 1950s, but the technical difficulties were too much to overcome. It was not until 1984 that the first 814-kilometer section of the railway, from Xining to Golmud, was completed, and the rest of the railway had to wait for the development of new technology.

The biggest issue was the permafrost. In the summer, in many places the top layer of the permafrost melts and turns to mud, making the ground unstable. A variety of solutions were used to get around this. In some cases, railway bridges were built. The longest bridge—a world record in fact—is over 11.7 kilometers in length. Railway bridges not

only keep the train line off the permafrost, but they also allow animals to pass under the tracks. In other cases, pipes were installed under the ground to keep it frozen during the summer. Finally, in some areas it was impossible to build the railway over the permafrost, so engineers tunneled through it.

It is hoped that many of the lessons learned from building the Qinghai-Tibet Railway can be used in a new project, linking Kashi (Kashgar), China with Islamabad, Pakistan along the Karakoram Highway, the highest highway in the world. This railway will travel 1,000 kilometers through the Pamir Mountains, which are nicknamed the Roof of the World because of their high elevation. While permafrost is not a factor on the Karakoram Highway, the road often gets damaged by winter landslides and large sections have to be rebuilt each spring. Building a railway along such a route will be a technical challenge indeed. It has not yet been announced when construction on this project will start.

Word Count: 349
Time: _____

Vocabulary List

accelerate *(4, 18, 20)*
accomplish *(2, 14)*
bid *(11)*
carriage *(2, 11)*
coal *(7)*
crow *(5, 20)*
drawback *(2, 13)*
dynasty *(7, 21)*
glory *(2, 11)*
grand *(2, 13, 15)*
hence *(9)*
initiative *(17)*
lengthen *(9, 10)*
levitation *(13)*
maglev *(13, 19, 20, 21)*
magnetic *(13)*
ministry *(14, 21)*
nickname *(9, 23)*
province *(2, 10)*
renaissance *(14)*
sheer *(2, 7, 13)*
silt *(11)*
sunflower *(11)*
venture *(14, 17, 20, 21)*
WiFi *(5)*
windowsill *(5)*